SCHOLASTIC EARLY SCIENCE

Rainy Days for Rabbit

Learn About the Weather

Kuntie Ramdat Balkaran

Illustrated by
Vandana Singh

SCHOLASTIC
New York Toronto London Auckland
Sydney New Delhi Hong Kong

'This weather is too hot,' said Papa Rabbit, coming back from the fields.

'The stream is just a trickle and the grass is brown.

I hope it rains soon.'

The sun's energy causes all weather changes on earth. The sun heats the atmosphere.
The atmosphere is the air around the earth, which is moved by winds.
Weather tells us about the atmosphere ... how hot, cold, wet, dry, calm, stormy,
clear or cloudy it is.

'I hate rainy weather!'
cried Little Rabbit.
'I don't like it when
it is muddy and wet.
I can't go outside to
play with my friends.'

'Do not complain about the rain,' said Mama Rabbit.

'Don't you know rain makes plants and trees grow? If there was no rain, we would have no food to eat and no water to drink!'

One raindrop is made up of millions of water droplets.
Water is needed for life, so every drop is precious.
Rain provides fresh water to many parts of the world.
Rain is always welcome after dry weather.

'There is always food in the farmer's garden,' said Little Rabbit, 'and water in his pond.

I think I will go check it out!'

Little Rabbit bounced across the field. He passed Turtle down by the stream.

'I'm going to munch on some lettuce leaves,' said Little Rabbit.

'Want to come with me?'

We use the same water over and over again, first as water, then as rain or snow or ice, then as water again.

'No, it's too hot,' replied Turtle.
'I hope it rains soon.'

The sun's energy melts snow and ice.

It heats water on the ground and in oceans, rivers, lakes and ponds.

Little Rabbit squeezed under the farmer's fence and gawked at the garden.

There was no lettuce, and the pond was dry. A few vegetables lay limp on the ground.

He met Duck on the way back.

'There is nothing to eat in the farmer's garden!' said Little Rabbit.

'I know. The sun has dried up everything. I hope it rains soon,' said Duck.

'I hate rain!' cried Little Rabbit. 'It's a nice day to play. Let's go find Turtle and Frog.'

Water dries up by changing into an invisible gas called water vapour.

Later, tired from playing all day, Little Rabbit crept home and snuggled down beside his mother.

'Mama, how come there are no stars out tonight?' he asked.

'The weather must be changing,' said Mama Rabbit.

'I'll go and have a quick look,' said Papa Rabbit.

Water vapour rises high in the sky where the air is cooler.

The cool air turns water vapour into an invisible mist.

The invisible mist turns into tiny droplets of water.

He poked his head out of the hole,
twitched his whiskers, and listened.
Then he hopped back into the burrow.

'The weather has changed indeed!' he cried.
'Clouds have rolled in.
That's why there are no stars!'

Water droplets stay in the air and form clouds, mist or haze.

When clouds are thick and dark, it means they are holding a lot of wate

'That's good news. Rainclouds will bring showers,' said Mama Rabbit. 'Soon there will be plenty to eat!'

'But where did the rainclouds come from?' asked Little Rabbit. 'It was hot and sunny all day.'

'No more questions tonight,' said Mama Rabbit. 'Tonight we will snuggle up in our cosy bed and listen for the patter of raindrops.'

But all they heard that night was the rumble of thunder far away.

The next morning,
Little Rabbit and Duck rushed down to the stream.
Turtle and Frog were already there,
watching dark clouds gather in the sky.

'Don't just sit and wait for the sun,'
cried Little Rabbit.
'Let's go have some fun!'

'Not today,' said Turtle.
'Today, we are waiting
for rain.'

Raindrops fall when the water gets too heavy for the clouds to hold.

Many raindrops start out as ice crystals in clouds.

If the ground is warm, the ice turns into water as it falls.

Raindrops inside storm clouds carry electricity.

When this electricity gets away, giant sparks flash across the sky.

This is called lightning.

'Listen. I will sing a rain song,' said Frog, and began to croak.

'Lightning will flash and then thunder will crash
and clouds will darken the sky.

Rain will pour down on each village and town.
No place on the ground will be dry!

Raindrops will fill up the streams and the brooks
And the rivers that rush to the sea.

Raindrops will fall on the fields and the hills,
on the lakes and the ponds and on me!'

Little Rabbit glared at the skies.
Suddenly,

SPLAT

A fat raindrop fell on his face.

Lightning jumps from the clouds to the earth, and then returns to the clouds.

Lightning makes the air so hot, it explodes with a very loud sound. This is called thunder.

Then
plop. Plip-plop.
Plop! Pi-shhhh-oooo!

The rain came tumbling down.

Little Rabbit raced for cover under a bush, as lightning lit up the skies and

KA-BOOM!

Thunder crashed overhead.

'Hurray for the rainstorm!' cried Turtle, as Duck and Frog frolicked in the field.

It rained for days.

Thunder rumbled and lightning forked the skies.

The stream swelled, the grass grew lush,

and the farmer's pond almost overflowed.

Lightning and thunder occur at the same time. But light travels faster than sound, so you see lightning before you hear thunder.

Finally, when the rain stopped, Little Rabbit looked out from his dry burrow.

'Oh, Mama! The grass is so green,' he cried.

'I can see flowers in the field!'

He also saw muddy patches and puddles,

but the sun looked lovely in the sky.

'Isn't it wonderful? The dry weather is over!' said Mama Rabbit.

'And now the sun is out. It always shines after the rain.'

'You are right, Mama,' said Little Rabbit.

He poked his head out of the rabbit hole, sniffed the fresh air, and called out to his friends.

The sun will heat the water on the ground and in oceans, rivers, lakes and ponds.

The water will change into water vapour, which will rise into the atmosphere.

Water vapour will form clouds and the water cycle will start all over again.

'When the field is dry, I will come out to play again!'

To Bob with love. KRB

Kuntie Ramdat Balkaran: Other picture books by Kuntie include *Mouse Sees the World, Little Monkey Gets Lost, A Cat Called Trouble Maker* and *Silly Dilly* (all Scholastic). Her first story, *A Pot of Money for Hard Times*, was the 2000 winner of a Canadian Writing for Children Competition. A former teacher, she now works in a special needs classroom in Winnipeg, Canada.

Vandana Singh: A dreamer and drawer, Vandana trained to be a pilot, a sculptor and became a film maker! A passionate animal lover, she is now anchored at WWF-India where her love of art and wildlife come together. She currently lives in Delhi in a snug apartment along with her three-legged dog who takes care of her.

Published by Scholastic India Pvt. Ltd.
A subsidiary of Scholastic Inc., New York, 10012 (USA).
Publishers since 1920, with international operations in Canada, Australia, New Zealand, the United Kingdom, India, and Hong Kong.

For information regarding permission, write to:
Scholastic India Pvt. Ltd.
A-27, Ground Floor, Bharti Sigma Centre
Infocity -1, Sector 34, Gurgaon 122001 (India)

First edition: August 2013
Reprint: November 2017, June 2018, January 2019

ISBN-13: 978-81-8477-682-9

Printed at Sterling Graphics Pvt. Ltd., Manesar